# I Died So I Could Live

## Wendy Shipman

**DEDICATION**

"My soul found a destination of peace

embodied in the aura of this man."

~I love you, Mark~

# ACKNOWLEDGEMENTS

**God**, I thank You! You have blessed me to author another book. Even though, I fought you hard against writing it, Your righteousness prevailed. And I did it by trusting in You.

**Mark**, my forever, there are too many things to name to thank you for. Just know, I appreciate you more and more as each day passes. I love you!

**Alexis**, thank you for allowing me to use a poem you wrote when you were in high school. I believe it was preordained because it so eloquently explains my story's ending.

**Rodney**, **Russell** and **Jessica L.**, thank you for all of your input. You are appreciated.

**Little Sister** – February 7, 2021! We do not owe NO ONE an explanation. I love you!

**Book Cover Design:** SelfPubBook.com/JayF

**Formatting by:** ebooklaunch.com

Arise [from spiritual depression to a new life], shine [be radiant with the glory **and** brilliance of the LORD]; for your light has come, and the glory **and** brilliance of the LORD has risen upon you.

~ Isaiah 60:1

*********************************************
## TRIGGER WARNING
*********************************************

The content included in this book includes mentions of real issues that you may be sensitive to, or unwilling to address ahead of time.

**Emotional Stress**

**Sexual Abuse**

**Miscarriage**

# INTRODUCTION

I kept wondering how I was going to start my story. It is in no way a glamorous depiction of my life. But it is my life – raw and transparent. Some may wonder why I am writing about the shame and the raw dealings I had in the past. Well... why not? I am here to talk about me and what I went through.

When I reached middle adulthood, I finally realized that I had to get rid of some of my shame to get my mind and heart in order to enjoy this precious life God gave me. By doing so, I wanted to share some of my hardships and maybe, just maybe, someone can relate to some of the things that I am about to share. My prayer is to have just one person who can relate to any chapter in my life and can know that you can overcome adversities and still have a prosperous life. It may not come when you want it to, but eventually it will come.

For those that really and truly know me, know that I suffer from major depressive disorder and panic/anxiety disorder. For those who did not know, I suppose you didn't know me as well as you thought. And that is ok because I never openly expressed myself to many people. As I got older, I wondered how did it get to this point? After many therapy sessions with my last two psychologists, I now know why. I went through several traumatic experiences over the years and I never got the much-needed counseling I should have received. Included in this book is my story and a few poems I had written when I was clinically depressed.

God allowed me to live fifty-one years in order to reach this point just to tell how I overcame. At the end of the book, you can get a better understanding of why I went through what I went through and experience that 'Ah-ha' moment when it all ties together. I hope that my book can reach someone who may have or are going through some of the same things that I went through. And by doing that, you can see how I was born to die just so I could live. And you can too.

# BARGAINING

I remember incredibly early on in my childhood that I never felt any kind of love from my mother. Love and compassion towards me were not standard. It was like everything I said and did, I got yelled at. And most of the time I did not even know why. I just basically accepted it because I guess in some disturbing way, I deserved it. Why would I be yelled at all the time if I did not deserve it, right?

My mother is an incredibly, beautiful woman. She is short in stature, under five feet tall, and always had gorgeous tresses. She also has a distinctive laugh. If you ever heard it, it would be one laugh that you would never forget. She is also a Gemini. I did not know about astrology back then. Today, I understand the two sides that this sign has. One minute they are fine, the next minute it is like they turn into a completely different person with a different personality. I would not call it bipolar, but a very noticeable distinction of two different people in one body. I wish I knew that then. I would have had a better understanding of why my Mother was the way she was. Anyway, she always made sure that I took care of myself the way a little girl should. Bathing, clean clothes, brushing my teeth... I was not going to be some nasty child under her roof. She would make sure that I had nice clothes and shoes to wear. People were not going to talk about her child as being unkept. No... this she would never allow.

As a young child to an adolescent teenager, love is what I needed. To me, love was not getting clothes and shoes. Love was not making sure my ribbons where neatly placed in my hair. In my opinion, those were basic needs. I needed that love where I heard my Momma say it to me – that verbal assurance. But I never got that from her. I guess by anyone else's viewpoint, it may be selfish of me. But materialistic things never meant love. I learned that incredibly early in life.

Whenever I wanted to talk to Momma about certain things, she always turned it into something negative and made me regret that I even asked, making me feel worse than I did beforehand. I mean, what was the point in even saying anything? All of the harsh 'shut-ups' and the 'hush your mouths' were enough to make anyone not want to talk any more. I became afraid to even ask questions for fear of being yelled at. So instead of asking or talking in general, I kept my feelings inside. I never could express any of my emotions for fear of rejection. So, when I became a teenager, I did just that. I got to where I did not even want to talk to anyone. I preferred keeping quiet as to avoid being scolded. What was the point in even holding conversations? I was never able to give my viewpoint in any kinds of discussions or arguments until I was much older. At the time, I could not express what I was feeling. So, I digressed into just not saying anything at all. Then she would get mad at me for that, too {sigh}. I did everything I could to try and please her. But, in the end it never seemed as if I could do anything right. It destroyed my soul, my spirit and my self-esteem. I felt unloved, unappreciated, unwanted and ugly.

As a young woman, I needed that love from my Mother in order to prosper from childhood to adulthood. Don't all daughters want to feel that way? There was even a time that I used to wonder if I was really her child. The way she belittled me in front of family and friends when she used to treat herself to libations was so embarrassing. I would secretly go somewhere and cry, but I made sure no one saw me so that I would not have to answer questions as to why my eyes were red. Do not get me wrong, she was never a heavy drinker. But when she was tipsy, it seemed like the contempt she felt for me came out a little more. The mean and hateful things that she used to say made me feel ugly – inside and out.

I always wondered if she was mad at the fact that when I was conceived, was she ready to be a mother? My mother was in her twenties when she had me, so she did not have me during her teenage years. She married my father, so it was not like she would have been an unwed mother. Did she even really want the responsibility of having a baby? I never asked. Honestly, I was and still am afraid to know what the answer may be.

Momma came from an extremely large family, even though she was an only child to my Grandmother. My Grandmother had eight siblings. Then those siblings had children. So, when the next generation of siblings had children, my cousins were several years older than I. I only recall about three or four that were around my age. Most of my family lived right there in Summerville, SC, but a few moved and lived in Connecticut. I was awfully close to my Grand Aunts, my Grandmother's sisters growing up. One Grand Aunt in particular, Aunt Pauline also known as Aunt Tee, was my favorite. She never had kids of her own, but you could never tell because she always treated everyone like they were her own children. Aunt Tee was the baker of the family – no, the community. Any cakes are pies that are needed, she was the one to call. I just remember whenever I needed that loving feeling from a woman, I could always depend on my Grandmother and Aunt Tee.

I do not ever recall Momma wanting to play or have any kind of fun with me. She worked a full-time job and took care of the house – just as any woman would do. She was also a very meticulous cleaner. Even today, you could eat off any floor in Momma's house. (I wish I had inherited that trait from her.) I think in a way, cleaning was a way to relax or to get things off her mind. So, she never had to time to play kids' games with me. My Grandmother used to play board games and cards whenever I asked. It was like she was my only friend instead of my elder.

There was a time when my Grandmother had to come and live with us. I was so happy because she was right in the room next to mine. Momma would get mad at me because I wanted to sleep in the room with my Grandmother. Being around her always made me feel safe. Somehow, though, it seemed like Momma was jealous of our relationship. I never understood how could she be jealous if she never wanted to spend time with me?

Even though it was the 1970s and 80s, my Grandmother still worked for white folks. She would literally walk 8 miles at least twice a week to cook and clean houses. Sometimes, she would be able to get rides to and from those houses. But if she couldn't, she walked. I was so angry and disappointed that she had to work like a slave at that day and age, but it was what she grew up doing and all she knew how to do. On the days my Grandmother had to work or was doing her own thing, I spent my time playing with my dolls or reading books. I was an avid reader at one time. It was nothing to read a 400-page book in one day. But reading did not take away the emptiness I felt inside. Reading helped to fill my mind with knowledge, but it did not fulfill my soul with the love I still desperately longed for. The one thing I never got from the one whom I needed from the most.

As I got older, I remember being so depressed with my life that I clung to music. Music, at a particular time in my life, was my therapy. Besides the books, music took me to a place of peace. I had a cousin who would always share his plethora of vinyl with me so that I could record it on my cassette player. Him sharing that love of music meant the world to me. I remember being so amazed at the abundance of music that was out there. I can still visualize the album covers of Teena Marie, Prince and The Jackson Five. It was like a music heaven made just for me. I used to play my same favorite songs several times in a row. I know my parents probably got tired of hearing the same songs over and over. But I was not bothering no one (except maybe them). I was in my own world. However, all the music on this earth could not keep me from thinking of ending my life.

It was right after middle school when I started to develop. You start to notice yourself and how others view you, too. As far back as I can remember, I have always had ugly feet. It is hereditary. I was dark skinned and at that time, dark skinned was not a 'thing' like it is now. Being that hue was not considered beautiful at all. And ever since one of my older cousins scolded me for repeating something her own daughter said, she ridiculed me and teased me about my 'buck teeth'. Those words were hot and scalding. It was at that moment in time when I really and truly did believe I was ugly. So along with not talking, I never smiled. Or if I did smile, I would cover my mouth. I started doing that long before there was a Celie in The Color Purple.

I was in a dark place in high school where I contemplated suicide. Feeling 'nothing' would have been better than the horrible feelings that were going around in my head. I was alone when it came to my emotions. I had no one to talk to about my secret thoughts. Nobody but the demons in my head that made me think that I was less than nothing. So really, "Who would have cared?". The only thing that 'saved' me from my demise was a book we read in 11th grade English class. In the book (which I cannot for the life of me remember the name), it talked about how people who committed suicide would go to hell. Not even sure if it was true at the time, but I had enough sense to know then hell was one place I know I did not want to go. I replayed that part of the book in my head over and over every night for weeks. I cried silently to God asking Him to please help me through this awful decision. I did not really want to end my life. I just wanted to end my situation. And I felt as if that was the only way to change it.

I remember crying to God one night, just sobbing uncontrollably, yet quiet enough for no one to hear me. I asked Him to please, change something in my life so I can be happy. I just wanted to be happy and pretty, that was all. I wanted to stop feeling sad all the time. I wanted Momma to stop yelling at me and to act like she really loved me. ***"Lord, if You can get me through this and I am able to have at least one child to carry on my name, You can do whatever You want with me. I am just so tired of feeling sad all of the time."***

Here I was bargaining with God like I was going through one of the five stages of grief. In a sense, I believe I was grieving. I died and I could not figure out how to live. I was not sure why having a child would have been a dealbreaker at that time since I was just an early teenager. But in my mind, I felt like I needed to have a child just so people could remember me. As I sit here and type, I remember it like it was yesterday. Back then, I thought more about having a namesake than I thought about my own life.

I did manage to get through the teenage years without harming myself. It was hard dealing with so many emotions that I could not express, not even to my Grandmother. I was so embarrassed to talk to anyone about my thoughts of suicide. I often wondered if I did have someone to talk to, would things have been different? I had a best friend since middle school and all through high school. We did just about everything together. I tried to spend as much time at her house as I could just to get away from my own home. But my parents did not want me to be a burden to another family. On the contrary, they did not make me feel like a burden. They treated me like I belonged there. I loved them. And I loved being around their family's dynamic. I saw the love my friend's Mom showed towards all of her children. Something I wanted so badly. And even with having a friend, I kept those feelings from her. I went through those difficult years by myself.

I did make it through high school. What a relief! I was still here and somewhat ready to embark on a different journey. I wanted and needed to find myself. My soul needed replenishing and repairing with something I was lacking. I was hoping that I could go out and find it on my own. In the meantime, it was time to get ready to go forward with my life.

When it was time to leave the nest, something miraculous happened. It was the very first time I heard my mother say, ***"I love you"*** to me. I was on my way to college at age eighteen. Yeah, eighteen years old. I always got the 'Love you' on the birthday cards and Christmas cards. But that is not the same as hearing someone close to you say those ever so meaningful words of endearment. So, at this point, after eighteen years, I did not believe her. Maybe she was just going through the motions of saying it because my Daddy said it. Or maybe it was because she was so elated, I was finally leaving the house and she would not have to deal with me anymore.

I did not know it then, but there was a valuable lesson that needed to be learned. At the end of the book, you will understand more about the revelations as to the 'why'. But I had to die internally at that time. My spirit, mentally and emotionally, had to experience that death to understand what was to become of my life.

**CHANGE**

Dear God,

Why do I feel so ugly? Is it because Momma called me
names?

Is it because my skin is too dark?

Is it because of my 'buck' teeth and deformed feet?

Why can't I get rid of these demons?

The adversary always had a way of making my Momma
degrade me.

I am not quite sure yet what it is that hurts worse.

Having Momma look and yell at me with disgust,

Or to have her tell me that I make her sick?

How can I tell my daughter to love herself

When I can't even look at my own worth in the mirror?

Lord, I am depending on You for change.

# DADDY'S GIRL

Growing up, I had a roller coaster of emotions and feelings I did not know exactly how to explain. But I do recall feeling overwhelmingly miserable and hopeless. They say that children can always remember the bad stuff that happened in their life. Don't get me wrong, some good things are remembered but it is the bad stuff that we often remember more than anything.

My Daddy was a tall, dark-skinned man with a head full of thick hair that would make any woman envious. I know I was. I, too, had thick hair, but not as beautiful as his. He took pride in his hair just like Solomon in the bible. Daddy always had a laid-back personality. He worked hard during the week, came home to watch his favorite television shows during the evenings and did not bother nobody. But drinking was his thing on the weekends. Hey, he was grown. If that was what he wanted to do during his free time, then that was what he was going to do. Who was going to tell him he couldn't?

All that mattered was where I stood in his life. I never had to doubt his love for me. Even when he drank, he told me that he loved me. He did not mind letting the world know that I was his daughter. He was proud of me and he let me know that; even if it was during one of his drinking moments, at least he said it. More importantly, I heard it and that was all that mattered. As a young girl going into womanhood, that is what I needed. Just to know that I was loved. Daddy was the very first man to love me and meant it.

Sometimes, I felt like the son he never had. Daddy took me just about everywhere he went, especially fishing. I supposed he would have taken me deer hunting too but getting up early was not my thing. And he probably thought it would have been too dangerous for me. However, I believe if I had mentioned to him that I wanted to go, I have no doubt that he would have taken me.

Back in the day, there were plenty of dirt roads in the area, so Daddy took me on them to learn how to drive. Sometimes, we would take Momma's car but most of the time, he would let me drive his black truck. He made driving fun and scary at the same time. I always watched him work under the car hood. He would show me how to fix things just in case I was ever by myself and needed to figure out what was wrong. I believe I knew more about a car by the time I graduated high school than most females my age.

I used to love to sit down and hear his stories of when he was younger. Some of them were heartbreaking, but at least he shared his life experiences with me. His sense of humor kept us laughing all the time. He would have his friends to come to the house and drink beer (some chose to bring their own hard liquor) in our yard under the tree. I would be in the midst listening and laughing, too. However, I knew my place when adults were talking. On a good weekend, he and Momma would fry chicken or fish and play music for our guests. Fortunately, there were not any close neighbors who would have been annoyed with the music. Sometimes, it would be well into the night before folks would start to leave. Those were some of the good memories that I have of my Daddy.

Daddy was well known around town. If they did not know who he was, he definitely knew who they were. He was born and raised in Summerville, SC, but had family in Lincolnville, Ravenel, St. Stephens and Moncks Corner. My family was everywhere. My Daddy worked for the school district in the Maintenance Department so it was very often that I would see him from time to time while I was attending school. If I saw him mowing the school lawn, I would make it a point to wave until he saw me. I could see his smile from far away and he happily threw up his hand to wave back. Some kids used to tease me because they saw my Daddy, but I was never embarrassed to see him. Seeing him always made me happy.

I even remember Daddy and I riding bicycles down to the Flowertown Festival one year. Depending on the direction we went, it was a good seven-mile drive from our house to the heart of the festival. Boy, was that exhausting. I would have done it every year if we could. But he said that was his first and last time doing that (lol). He loved to be on the go but not by bicycle. He was not a person who liked to stay home all the time. Daddy was happy to have me tag along, too. I would go anywhere just to get away from home.

When Daddy found out that I decided to take NJROTC in high school, you talk about a proud man? I only took that class for a year but just knowing I enrolled in the class was enough for him. He never served in the military, but he loved hearing me talk about the field trips out in the Charleston Harbor and me shooting at the gun range. He was so proud that I could shoot a gun and not be afraid to use it. I am telling you… I should have been a boy.

As wonderful as everything sounds, Daddy was not a perfect man. The very things that I loved my Daddy for are the same things another woman love him for, too. It was not until I was in my early teens, I found out that I was the 'excuse' to go play with some little girls my age around the block. And while I was playing, he was too. Rumor had it that all of that playing produced a child. No one, not Daddy and especially not Momma, wanted to talk to me about this little girl. There was a time when I used to play with her all of the time. Then things stopped with no explanation to me as to why. I spent years and years agonizing as to what the truth was, but no one was courageous enough to tell me. I was told more lies than truths.

That whole ordeal had me so hurt and ashamed of what my Daddy put Momma through. I can assure you; she was hurt from the accusations, and rightfully so. I was embarrassed for my Momma and even I was harassed by people, mostly the neighborhood kids, who came to me regarding this child. I was always on Momma's side when it came to this matter. No woman should have to deal with a spouse's deceitful ways. I, at one point, told Momma that she should leave Daddy. Forget all of the 'I stayed because of the kids' mess that women were so quick to say. My Mother was resilient and strong and could have done it on her own. But she decided she was not about to let anyone destroy the home she built. That, and the fact that Daddy begged her not to leave him, is why she stayed. Still, it was a very virtuous thing for her to do and still be able to hold her head up. So, throughout that entire situation, it was something between Momma, Daddy and the other woman. I and the other little girl just so happened to be caught up in the middle somewhere. On one hand, I believed this little girl could have really been my sister, but on the other hand I was adamantly told she wasn't. And because of the things I was told and was not told, I never had a relationship with her. At the end of this book though, you will find out what happened to this little girl.

My Daddy never, ever hit me. Momma did all of the beatings. (Looking back now, I believe those beatings were meant for Daddy, but I was an easier target.) Even though Daddy was very mellow, he still intimidated me. I tried my best to never disappoint him because I did not want him to NOT love me. The summer we found out that he was diagnosed with leukemia, I did not want to believe it. It took that first stay at the hospital and the first bag of chemo for that realization to really sink in that this is real. After a three-year battle with leukemia including two remissions, his death shook me to the core. I was well into young adulthood when he passed. When my Daddy left me, I died inside. What hurt me most of all was the fact that I could not attend his funeral. He died on a Sunday and I had given birth to my daughter on Monday, the next day. If only Momma could have waited until Thursday, just one day, I could have attended his funeral. I needed that closure with my Daddy and to say good-by to him one last time. Just one day. She didn't. The funeral was on Wednesday. Daddy was her husband. I did not even have a say in the matter. It was her choice when she wanted to bury my father. So, it was done.

I have spent the last twenty-four years mourning the first man that every loved me. The first man who loved me unconditionally The first man who would have gone to the ends of the earth just for me. Gone. To this day, I miss him so much it hurts. I just want to be able to tell him all the good and bad things that have happened in my life. I wish he could see how the world has turned out since he left us twenty-four years ago. I wish he could have met 'Lucky' when she was born. He would have seen how incredibly bright and intelligent she grew up to be. His chest would have been swollen with pride to know she became a Registered Nurse, a woman with such a beautiful soul and personality. And a Grandson who is as equally bright and intelligent ... seeing him play football in high school and being Defensive Player of the Year in the same county he worked for fifteen years, his heart would not have been able to take all of it in.

More importantly, I wish he could have met the man that has made my life so happy and peaceful. I know for a fact that he and my now husband would have gotten along very well. Two country boys with a love of sports and the gift of gab! I probably would have been jealous of their relationship as in-laws. Daddy would have also gained another grandson who plays basketball in high school. Something else he would have been proud of. However, life has moved on and so did I.

## Leukemia

Leukemia? "Oh, no! That cannot be true!
You have too much LIFE still inside of you.
You took me places I have never gone.
You told me many things, so I'll never go wrong."

Leukemia? "No, Daddy, they made a mistake."
That Doctor said, "Drink plenty of fluids, you'll be ok."
He said, "I know, baby, but the hospital ran plenty of tests.
There is no mistake, time to let God do the rest."

Leukemia? You don't know who you are dealing with.
My Daddy is strong, and he wants to live.
This pain and fatigue won't keep him down.
Many people would say they still see him around town.

Leukemia? I had no idea what he had to go through.
Chemotherapy, platelets, and transfusions ... who knew?
Weight loss, hair loss and your teeth are gone, too.
Daddy, this disease sucked the life right out of you.

Leukemia? God ... no, no, no ... please don't take him away.
My daughter, his first grandchild, will be born the very next day.
"Daddy, you can't leave me now, we still have so much to do.

And do you want Momma to spoil your Grandbaby
without you?"

Leukemia? Daddy is gone and I could not say good-bye.
I was in the hospital trying to decide.
Should I leave to go tell you one last time
How much I love you, I will miss you, and have one last
cry?
But you would say "No! Stay there and take care of
yourself.
You are a Momma now. And besides, you will need your
rest."

Leukemia? My Daddy lost the fight, and you won the
war.
But I am older now, no need to keep score.
It took years and years to get over my loss.
And eventually, God willing, again our paths will cross.

# SERPENT EYES

I had hoped that college would have given me a sense of happiness by being independent and being on my own, per se. I needed to find happiness by making new friends while meeting new people. The one college that I wanted to go to messed up my financial aid and truthfully, made me feel like they did not have my best interest at heart. So, I ended up at a college that was more professional. They made me feel like they really wanted me as a student. However, this school was not my first choice.

I was expecting a great life changing experience. What I did not know though was that depression was going to follow me like a bad zit that always comes out on the middle of your forehead. You know it is coming, just not sure when it will pop up. Yet, I tried my best to overlook the bad in order to find myself. I lost the first eighteen years of my life, so this was a chance to enjoy life experiences away from home. I kept an open mind to accept anything.

I joined a Gospel Choir at the University and enjoyed it so much. We were able to go to different places to sing all the while doing something that I loved... listening to music. Although that was fun, depression still had a hold of me. I had to worry about paying for the college. Although Momma and Daddy did not make a lot of money, in the government's eyes, two working parents should be able to afford to pay my tuition. That was not the case at all. So not only did I have to get loans, but I also had to do work-study and work part-time just to attend. And working all the time did not mix at all while trying to study.

This is the crazy part. When I first got accepted to this institution, they said that the scores from my SATs were not high enough. Therefore, I was placed into remedial English (imagine that?). Now to me, remedial means you are having difficulty or a slower than the average time reading and writing. That took a toll on my self-esteem. It was like **'Hey you know you're not as good as everybody else, so you have to start at the bottom'.** In high school, I was an average student but because I spent my time depressed, I never excelled like I could have. So, because of my low SAT scores, I had to take this remedial class before I could even get into 101. It was discouraging to say the least. But I chose to make the best of a humiliating situation. No one knew except me and my professor. I looked at it like another failure added to my list of life experiences.

My roommate in college was my best friend in high school. We did everything together. Two peas in a pod. You did not see one without the other. I spent so many great times with her before and after high school. Putting aside the academic situation, the student life was fantastic. Being able to walk around this huge campus, to come back to the dorm whenever we pleased, attending fraternity and sorority house parties, free tickets to the football games ... it was a little like heaven on earth. It felt so good to laugh and enjoy myself.

A few weeks into the semester, I met a guy named Curtis that seemed like he was interested in me. Now, one thing about me ... I was never one to step up and talk to guys for fear of rejection. I was told later in life that I always had a 'stand-offish' look on my face. I never realized it, but I guess I did because I heard it from more than one person. But thinking back, I supposed there was a rhyme to my reason for the look. I never felt pretty or worthy enough for anyone to talk to me. My face was my personal defense mechanism that said to just leave me alone.

Anyway… back to this 'nice' guy. I had seen him around campus a few times. We always spoke whenever we passed by each other walking to or from class. Sometimes, we would stop briefly to talk about our day, then go about our separate ways. This one Sunday afternoon the campus was deathly quiet. Students were either hungover from the night before or home for the weekend. My roommate went out for the day and I was in the room by myself. Curtis called my room phone, asked if I was doing anything and could he come by my room? I was not doing anything, so I said sure, why not? Fortunately, I stayed in a dorm where no one could just come up as they pleased. They had to be signed in by someone who lived in the dorm.

I met Curtis downstairs and signed him into the book as a visitor. When he came in, he complimented our dorm room and how 'homey' it looked. We sat and laughed for a little while. I noticed that he was fidgeting in his seat but thought nothing of it. Then he asked about my roommate and where was she. I told him that she was out for the day and would not be back until later. Instantaneously, his demeanor changed. The first thing I noticed was his eyes. The shape of his eyes looked almost 'serpent' like. Then his body language shifted. The shape of his eyes had me so distracted, I lost focus of my surroundings. Before I could react to the sudden movement in front of me, his hands gripped the tops of my arms and he forcibly pressed my body against his. I managed to snap out of my trance and say, "What are you doing?" before his mouth was on mine. I remember him saying something about 'I really like you,' 'you are mine' and 'I've been waiting on this". And then he started kissing me again. As I struggled to wiggle my arms away from him to push him off of me, the stronger his grip grew. The next thing I knew, he manhandled me across the bed. I tried to fight him off, but he was too strong and overpowered my little 120 lbs. 5'4" self. When watching movies, I never understood how a woman could not fight off their attacker - until now. Shocked and in disbelief that this was really happening, all I could do was hope that he did not beat me up or kill me. The way I felt with the thickening, swollen feeling of vomit in my throat, he might as well had. I suffocated internally because what he just did killed the spirit inside of me. Right there on my bed, I died.

After it was over, he stood up and looked at me. Smiling, he said, "That was great. I will let myself out. See you later." And just like that, he was gone. I laid there motionless and traumatized. I could not scream. If I screamed, I would have shattered into pieces. I felt embarrassed, dirty and betrayed. I let this guy into my room, and he treated me like a tramp he met out in the streets. I was a nothing to him. I felt like nothing. So, who is going to believe he raped me? Seriously, who would have believed me? I cried in a fetal position for at least forty-five minutes. At one time, I wished I did die so I would not have to tell anyone what happened to me. I did not ever want to think about what I fool I was to trust this guy. But God would not let me die. I kept on breathing. Even when I secretly held my breath, hoping my heart would stop. God pushed the air out of lungs just so I could breathe again.

I got up slowly because soreness had started to really set in once the adrenaline wore off. I put on a robe and walked down to the community hall bathroom and showered. I know I stood in there at least fifteen minutes before I finally washed off the filth from my body. I went back to my room and threw the comforter and the sheets on my bed into a trash bag. Thankfully, I had an extra comforter to use so when my roommate came back to the room, it just looked like I changed my bedding. I never told her of this day. I never told anyone how this guy stole the core of what little essence I had of myself. All the shame and the guilt I withheld to myself. I had to. Who was I going to tell?

Since that incident occurred, the next two years of my college life snowballed. I spent my days working just to get away from my room. I could not study because mentally and emotionally, my head was not in it. Consequently, it reflected in my grades. I went on academic suspension and ended up going back to the very place I wanted to get away from. Home.

# FROZEN

When I was 21 years old, I worked at a men's retail store in the mall. Since I did not finish college, I needed to work so I started off at a clothing store for the classy and elite women. I was so bored, but it paid the bills. One day, a young woman my age walked into the store. She was a very pretty and had the brightest smile. Her name was Jackie, and she was a manager at another store in the mall. I guess she could tell that I was un-happy where I was. She offered me a full-time position at her store if I wanted to do something different. It was a no-brainer... I accepted immediately. I was so glad for another opportunity that I was not even looking for at the time.

After completing my two weeks' notice and hateful glares from my old manager, I was happily ready for my new endeavor. It was a completely different atmos-phere. Instead of the dreadful elevator music I heard day in and day out at the old job, I was able to listen to my favorite radio station at the new one. That right there was everything! And it was not long, just a few weeks, before I became an assistant manager.

I had a great working relationship with my new boss, Jackie. To this day, she was one of the best man-agers I had ever worked for. That is so important in any job. She not only trusted me after only a few weeks, but she also believed in my abilities to get the job done. And it proved to be even more of a blessing as the years went by because that is the same work ethic that I car-ried with me at every job I was ever assigned.

Jackie was so down to earth … we talked as if we were sisters and hung out at the clubs like best friends. From time to time, we would even go to the Food Court to have lunch while the part-time workers would watch the store. Once every blue moon, we would indulge in a drink during work hours. That was the best part about being young and adventurous. When we got back to work, we would just giggle and laugh some more at the looks our part-timers would give us. I admired her beautiful personality as well as the beauty she was. She was a great teacher, showing me the ins and outs of the business. Men's clothing was amazingly simple. It was a very trendy shop that had a very heavy traffic flow. And because the Navy Base was docked in the town we worked in; it was a constant 'sale heaven'. She would tell me who the best clients were and the ones who only came there to 'look' at the help. Men will be men.

I started seeing this Navy guy named Bryson. He was tall, carried himself with a model-like stature and very charming. He was smooth and very charismatic. We never actually became a couple. He was a little too 'pretty' for me. So, we just enjoyed each other's company from time to time. And just when I felt that he only wanted the pleasure instead of the complete package, I slowly began to make excuses why I could not meet up with him. But to be on the safe side, I decided to call my gynecologist to start me on birth control pills - just in case. No questions asked, the doctor called in a prescription to get me started.

Two weeks before my 22nd birthday, I started taking the birth control pills. Not knowing what to expect, other than what the information leaflet told me, I was on my own. After my first week on the pills, I noticed that I did not stop menstruating. Some days it would slow down like it was going to stop. Then it would start up again like it just started. I could not figure out what was going on. I called my doctor and he said that sometimes when you start a birth control pill, it can mess with your hormones and I should not worry. It would stop on its own.

My birthday came, then it went. Although I was glad to have another birthday, I was miserable and exhausted. I had a cycle for three straight weeks. Jackie was very understanding of what was going on. A little too understanding as I found out later. I tried extremely hard not to miss work because of how I was feeling. But this one evening changed everything. It was me and a part-time worker for the evening at the store. I had terrible pains in my stomach. The menstrual cramps were constant, and I was in severe pain. Thankfully, it was a quiet night in the mall, so I told my coworker to watch the store while I went to the back to use the restroom. As I made it to the bathroom, I sat on the toilet and pulled out my tampon. I literally heard a 'gush', but it was not urine flowing. The gush was so much so - I was afraid to look. Another pain hit but this time, it was sharp and searing. I leaned forward. Then, I felt a small, soft object come outside of me.

Oblivious to my naivety, still not realizing what just happened, I was too scared to stand up and look in the toilet. Still cramping slightly, I managed to slowly lift myself up. What I saw literally took my breath away. I could not inhale or exhale for a couple of seconds because my lungs froze. Then I gasped, "OH MY GOD!" Staring back at me was a translucent shaped kidney bean with distinctive black circles on the top of its skin. I was looking at a fetus. My fetus. I was too shocked to cry. I was too numb to call for help. I just stood there... and stared.

I am not sure if it was a 'motherly' instinct, but I could not bring myself to flush the toilet. I looked around and grabbed some clean gloves out of the box underneath the bathroom sink and did the unthinkable to some, but the right thing to others. I picked up my baby out of that toilet and put it inside of a small empty jar I found in the bathroom. I filled it with water, sealed it and hid it under my coat until it was time for me to go home. Time got away from me and I do not know how long I was gone. I really did not care. But it was long enough for my co-worker to ask me if I was ok. I lied and said I was.

When I got home, I laid awake most of the night, still not believing what happened only hours before. The cramping that I felt before was no longer there. Even the bleeding came to a minimal trickle. I held in my hand the jar with the kidney bean inside. I just stared at my baby for what seemed like hours. Its life came to a complete stop. I would never get to see what or who it would have looked like had it been born at full term. I never even knew if it was a boy or girl. My mind was spinning, and the tears were streaming. I held my child all night because I knew this would have been the last time I could hold it in my hands.

The next day, I requested an emergency visit to my primary care doctor. I carried a small paper bag into the office with me. I was so embarrassed and ashamed of what I handed to him. As I handed him the bag, I broke down into tears because I would never see my little kidney bean again. The look in his eyes was sheer shock as he took the jar outside of the patient room. He came back and verified with me that it was indeed a fetus, at least 8 weeks old. I explained to my primary doctor of my call to the GYN doctor who prescribed the birth control. He questioned me if the doctor tested me first.

"No."

I was told if the gynecologist had seen me first before prescribing the birth control, he would have known to tell me then that I was already pregnant. Taking the birth control is what contributed to me losing the baby. My baby.

Not only did my baby die... I died too.

My primary doctor immediately scheduled an emergency D & C just in case there were any remaining tissues in my uterus. Fortunately, everything was flushed out when the miscarriage happened. Now I understand why there was so much continuous blood and immense cramping. My body was rejecting my baby because of me. For a long time, I blamed myself for losing this baby. I should have known. Even though I was in the beginning of the first trimester, as a woman, I should have known. Although, I had nothing - no nausea, no vomiting, no nothing. But still - I should have known.

It was a few days afterwards that I told Bryson about what happened to me. I could not tell if his concern was genuine or just a passive sigh of relief. Either way, I did not care. I could not react to anything he was saying. I just wanted him to know about the miscarriage and to be left alone. I knew he did not genuinely care about me because the following weekend, he wanted to do more than just 'see' me. Disgusted that he would completely ignore my feelings, the changes my body went through and the loss that I felt (we should have both felt) afterwards, I completely deleted him from my life. And sometime shortly thereafter, his ship sailed away from the area. I never heard from him again.

The pain of losing something so precious as a baby, already growing and nurturing inside of me, one I never got the opportunity to know and love, was unbearable. I questioned God as to why this happen to me? Why was my life so filled with agonizing disappointments? Life continued and so did I. I finally had to ask Jackie for some time off so my body and mind could heal from that life changing event. When I told her what happened (not mentioning where it happened), she approved immediately. Never going into any details, she said she 'understood'. And even through all of that, I never pursued counseling for the loss of my baby. I dealt with the hand I was given by myself. And I never sought legal counsel against the doctor who gave me the birth control before checking me. During that time, I had no one to help or support me with legal issues nor did I have the finances for it. It took me a while to forgive my doctor for what happened. It took even longer to forgive myself.

I can completely understand how people can 'forget' certain hurtful events in their lives. I did. Because of how painful it was and the unbelievable the way it happened; I blocked that part of my life out of my head. It is a blur. Every now and then when I look at my oldest, I think about the fact that I could have had another child six years older than her. But God knew what was best. The way it happened was the way God intended it to be.

# Blessings from Big Regrets

In 1995, I met my oldest children's father when I was doing well for myself. I had been working at a great job for four years and living alone. I had no complaints other than feeling incredibly lonely. It just so happened to be a holiday weekend, so I decided to get my car serviced. He came walking into the waiting area shortly after I did. After chit-chatting with him, he seemed like an alright kind of guy. My 'Spidey Senses' were tingling, but since I had not been dating anyone at the time and I thought I knew what I was getting into, I assumed maybe it was just the anxiety of meeting someone new. Years later, my 'Spidey Senses' were on point. But by then, it was too late.

Months went by and things were going ok. Then some unfortunate circumstances came into play and he came to live with me. He could have left the area to go back to his hometown out of state, but I cared about him and honestly did not want him to leave. So, I offered him to stay with me. He said he would help with some of the bills at my place. At the time, he was attending his last year in college and working a part-time job that paid minimum wage. I was ok with that if he was able to pay his portion of the bills. Well, if the cable bill was $59.36, I was fortunate if I got $25. I know it was not half. And I know he was working part-time. However, he was not making any extra effort to do his part either. There were times when I did not get anything at all. It was then I began to pick up on 'things' that those rose-colored glasses kept me from seeing.

I got pregnant at the beginning of 1996. I had also received a promotion from my job. It entitled me to live in Columbia, SC - all expenses paid. Since it was only ninety minutes away, I was able to keep my place in my hometown. While I spent my first few months away from home, I was overcome with loneliness and morning sickness. He, on the other hand, was at my place living like a king. I imagine that is how I would have felt if I barely spent money on paying bills while living basically free of charge. I blame only myself for this set up. I knew better but loneliness overshadowed ALL of my common senses.

By this time, my Grandmother had moved away from my old house and moved into an apartment building right across from me. It was a very small apartment community where two of my Grand Aunts stayed in the building also. One Friday evening, I decided to travel home instead of staying in Columbia. I had an awfully bad dream the night before and my spirit just did not sit right with me. When I arrived home, I went straight to my place instead of stopping by my Grandmother's house. I wanted to unwind a little before seeing anyone.

When it dawned on me that I did not talk to her yet, it was around seven or eight in the evening. I called her phone. No answer. I called again. Still no answer. I peeped out of my window and could see the television light illuminating from her living room window. Still, thinking nothing of it, I put on some clothes to go knock on her door. Still there was no answer. I went to her bedroom window and tried to see if I could see her walking around. There … on the bathroom floor … that cannot be … trying to focus my eyes through the lace curtains … was my Grandmother. Knocking on the window and yelling out her name, I was in full panic mode. I ran to my Aunt's house and told her to call 911. The ex heard the commotion and ran downstairs to see what was wrong with me. I showed him what I saw in the window and he knew she was gone. But I did not want to believe it. No sooner than he told me to calm down, the police arrived. The police had no other choice but to break the door down. The ex followed the police officer. He came back out and told me she was gone.

No! No! No! No! No!

Why didn't I stop by to see her when I first got home? I should have known… the dream. The old folks used to say if you dream about blood, it means death. I dreamed about my own Grandmother's death and I did not get a chance to see her before … Oh my God! If only I had stopped by on my way up to my place, I would have seen her. I would have had a chance to talk to her. I would have laid my eyes on her before God took her away. I will forever regret that missed opportunity to indirectly say good-by.

The guilt ate away at me for weeks. And for weeks, for some reason, I was scared to look out of a window when it was dark. I was afraid I was going to see her face looking back at me. After about a month of living in 'fear' she finally came to me in a dream. In the dream, I dropped down to me knees and told her that I was afraid to look at her because I was afraid of what I would see. My Grandmother came to me, placed her loving arms around me and told me not to every be afraid again. Immediately, the weight was lifted off and I cried myself awake. The peace I felt after that night not only helped me but the baby I was carrying inside.

It seemed as if the death of my Grandmother took a toll on my Daddy, too, because he came out of remission for the second time and the leukemia came back. Therefore, I gave up my once in a lifetime opportunity in Columbia to move back home. Dealing with my Grandmother's death, being pregnant and Daddy being sick was too much for me to handle alone in another city.

Even though Daddy was not doing well, he along with Momma and the ex came to Columbia to get my things to come back home. Once I got back, there was finally some normalcy in my life. I went back to my old job and spent countless days going to see my Daddy in the hospital. One thing was for sure. He was so ready to see 'Lucky'. When I first told him that I was pregnant, he was so excited to have his first grandchild. I was twenty-seven at the time so he thought he would never get the chance. To this day, I never knew why he called her Lucky.

My pregnancy with my daughter was remarkably easy. I suppose the fact that I kept moving, kept waddling down the Oncology Floor helped. In my spiritual sense, I believe that my Daddy took away a lot of the misery from me that sometimes accompany pregnancy. At the time, the ex did not cause too much emotional stress on me because I had my Daddy to look out for me. I felt no anxiety when my Daddy was in my life. It was then, when God took him away, that the strain of my reality began. The first man who loved me was gone. And the man (who would later marry me) promised my Daddy that he would fill my Daddy's shoes by taking care of me. This man failed miserably.

God blessed me with an angel the day after my Daddy passed. Momma took me to the doctor's office, then to the hospital after confirming I was indeed in labor. I think her waiting for the baby was better than her reality that her husband of 28 years was gone. But she stayed the entire time. She even held my daughter minutes after she was born. I saw her smile during her moment of grief. I, on the other hand, thought my heart would literally explode either from the pain of death or the joy of life ... or both. Such a beautiful little girl who came at a time that I needed her the most. God works that way sometimes. I spent hours just looking at her with tears streaming down my face. She did not know how much of a blessing she was to me. I gave her life, but what she did not know was that SHE WAS my life.

After the birth, it seemed as if the ex gave excuse after excuse as to why he could not find a job in our area. So, he accepted a job in Columbia which was an hour and a half away. Looking back on it now, it was just an excuse from handling the responsibilities of being a father. A man who is serious about his family will do what is necessary, but technically, I was not family. We were not even married at that time; just engaged. His daughter should have been his first priority. But as soon as he got a 'chance to getaway' card, he was gone. Leaving behind the responsibilities of two parents to fall on me alone.

I must admit, it was hard the first few months with the baby. But I had great support from my Aunt Tee. She kept the baby while I worked. Aunt Tee was home alone at the time so having a baby around was great company for her. However, when my Momma found out about this arraignment, I think she became a little jealous because her granddaughter was not around as much. It was not like I did not ask. When I did ask for help, I would get the "yeah, I guess" and the "we'll see" answers. I did not have time for that and could not depend on maybes. So, I asked someone who wanted to help without questioning. I knew my Aunt Tee and my daughter would have been great together. When I was pregnant and my daughter heard my Aunt's voice, she would try and jump out of my belly. She knew my Aunt's voice more than anyone else's.

Fast forwarding a little less than two years later, I married the ex. and moved to Columbia away from family. Basically, I let him sweet talk his way back into my life. I got bamboozled but I try my best not to live by regrets because I got pregnant again. My second child, a son, was my miracle baby. After being off birth control for a year, I thought I was not able to have any more children. After conception, my son went through so much stress in the womb because of the emotional and mental abuse I received from his father. It was noticeably clear at that time the ex did not care about me or my well-being. I recall a time when he asked me to help him put up a shed in the back yard. He had me hold the siding or pole up while he would screw or drill in holes. And when I complained that my back and groin was hurting, he would get mad. Mind you, I was about 6 to 7 months pregnant. I was out there all day with him (while still trying to keep my daughter occupied inside the house) until it turned dusk. I felt so stupid and naïve to have even go out knowing my condition. Especially since he could have asked one of our male neighbors to help. It goes to show just how much he thought of his pregnant wife's condition versus getting the shed up. The shed was a priority. Again, my common sense obviously was not in working commission. My body hurt for days after that.

When I moved to Columbia after marriage, I brought with me my expenses, which really was not much since I was doing well financially. But after moving, there were extra rent monies and daycare fees due. Trying to help take care of family needs caused me to get behind on my already established bills. It got so bad that I had to file bankruptcy. Not only did it ruin my credit, but my car was also repossessed. The ex's response, "That's on you. They were your bills." Even though he willingly indulged in everything I bought with my money, sat and laid down on all the furniture I bought, somehow everything was all my responsibility. I felt so betrayed because he never once said **"I got you"**. I was always in this marriage alone.

These few examples along with the stress of dealing of other women were devastating. I tried to maintain a sense of composure because I was carrying my son as well as burdens I had no business bearing. I was always hurting and sick all the time, nothing like my first pregnancy. I know that if my Daddy were alive and had any clue of what was going on with me, he would have come to the house with his pickup truck and said, **"Let's go!"** And I would have already had me and my daughter's things already packed and we would be waiting by the road. But I stayed. What a trooper I was! Nahhh... more like a fool staying with a man that did not give a damn about me.

# YOU LEFT ME

The ex, our daughter and I went to visit my hometown for the day. It was just a day trip to spend time away from our home. It was nighttime, maybe around 10 p.m., when we decided to make that 90-minute drive back to Columbia. We were twenty minutes away from Momma's house when we got a flat tire on the interstate. My ex had a hard time getting the lug nuts off the rim because it needed a key in order to unlock. We were basically stuck on the side of the road.

Back in 1999, there were cell phones, but we did not have one with us. Therefore, we could not call anyone to help. At that time of night, there were not many travelers on the road. I tried not to show fear in front of my daughter. She was only three at the time and did not need to see Mom afraid. I had her come sit on my lap in the front seat, trying to keep her warm because it was a cool October night.

About an hour passed after sitting in the car when a Highway Patrol car driving on the opposite side of the road made a U-turn and came up behind us. The female officer stopped because she saw the emergency blinkers on the car. Thank God. She allowed me to call my mother on her car phone in the patrol car. That way Momma could come and pick us up to go back to her house and we would worry about getting the car the next morning. I walked to the patrol car and called my mother. I already knew what kind of reaction I would get, but I needed my daughter out of that unsafe environment. I called because I did not know anyone else who could help. As I proceeded to tell Momma the exact location of where we were, I could tell by her lack of concern in her voice that this was not going to have a good ending. I verified with the Officer and explained to her that we were a few miles pass the specific exit number. She could not miss us because ... well ... we had the only car on the side of the road with blinkers on. Reluctantly, she agreed to come and get us. So, we waited. We thanked the Officer and told her that we would just wait for my Mother to come and pick us up. It was not going to take thirty minutes for her to get to us, so I wrapped my daughter in my arms and let her fall asleep until her Granny arrived.

One hour passed by. I was pissed. Then, two hours passed by. By this time, the ex (who always tried to remain cool during tumultuous situations) was pissed, too. He said that we could not sit in this car all night and said we needed to walk to the next exit. This was past midnight. Considering the circumstances, staying in the vehicle at that time of night was not safe. I thought more about my daughter than I did myself, so I agreed. The ex got the tire iron from the trunk of the car in case we needed some sort of protection. So, as I held on tight to my daughter's hand, the three of us started walking down I-26 after midnight on a Sunday morning. We made it about a quarter of a mile down the road when we saw a car on the other side of the interstate make a U-turn. The car slowly approached behind us and two women called out from inside of the car. They said they saw us walking and asked if we needed a ride to the next exit. It was by the Grace of God that 1) these women really wanted to help, 2) they did not want to kill us, and 3) they were willing to drive us because that mile turned out to be two miles ahead. We all got into the car (the ex still with the tire iron in his hand) and headed to the next exit. They talked about just coming from a nightclub. Although I was still angry, disappointed and exhausted, I managed to make small talk letting them know I knew which nightclub they were talking about. We were so thankful and grateful that those two angels took us safely to the gas station. I wish I knew who they were... to tell them how thankful I still am that they saved us that night.

When we got to the gas station, we ran into the same Highway Patrol Officer that helped us on the interstate just two hours before. She was just as surprised to see us as were seeing her. She asked what happened and my ex went on to explain that my Mother never came. By this time, my embarrassment level surpassed my anger level. The Officer asked if we wanted to use her phone again. I could not make myself go to the phone. So, I didn't. The ex called my Mother and asked her why she never came? When the ex came back into the store, he told me that she said she could not find us, so she went back home.

**"WHAT?"**

So, what you are saying to me is that she did not think enough or cared enough of her pregnant daughter and three-year-old granddaughter to look for us until we could be found?

At that moment, I died.

How humiliating! How hurtful and demeaning I felt in front of the ex and the police officer. My own mother turned around and went back home because she could not find us. What Mother would think of doing that? I would NEVER, EVER leave my child, I do not care how old he or she is, on the side of the road. I would search until I found him or her. I would not care if it took days, I could never do that to any of my children. But I suppose, I just was not worth it to her. I never was. Not sure what made me think otherwise, but foolishly, I did.

In the meantime, the Officer called a tow truck to come and they were to come to the rescue. They had to break the lug nuts in order to change the tire and were finally able to put on the spare. We were still an hour and ten minutes away from our home. Momma's house was closer. We could have just gone back to her house to get a few hours of sleep.

No. Let's just make this long drive back home.

**You Left Me**
Close to midnight
Out in the dark on the side of the road
Eight months pregnant with a three-year-old child
Husband protecting us with a tire iron
**You left me.**

I called you
Where are you because I am waiting
It's cold and uncomfortable
My child is tired and afraid of the dark
**You left me.**

We started walking
The three of us on Interstate 26
Picked up by God's travelling angels, protecting us
Shielding us from imminent danger
**You left me.**

You said
You could not find us, so you turned around and went
back home
You didn't even look for us out in the dark
You didn't love me enough to come and find me
**You left me, Momma ... out there.**

# WHEN GOD SAID GO

Have you ever been cheated on by your spouse or your significant other? It is the most disrespectful, degrading feeling to ever experience. It makes you feel less than a woman to know that your husband - You know the one who is supposed to love you by forsaking all others? - preferred seeking pleasure outside of the home. And when they lie about it, it just adds fuel to the fire.

I always believed in God and the sanctity of marriage. I never wanted to get divorced. I wanted to live that happily ever after with my spouse. I wanted to grow old and be able to spoil our grandchildren together. But instead, besides the children, I got nothing but emotional abuse, mental stress and disappointments.

I had always been a person who tried to live by the 'Golden Rule' and by God's Word as much as humanly possible (He is still working on me). I did not want to go against my vows. Every word that I said before God, I meant – for better and for worse. So, when my ex decided to step out of the marriage, I was devastated. Consider me a fool, but I still did not give up. I recommended marriage counseling to salvage our relationship. But when you only come to one out of four sessions, obviously he was too far gone, and his mind was made up. He did not want me. Not only was it disrespectful, but it was also embarrassing for me to show up alone.

Yet still, I kept trying. This time, I turned to my church's Pastor for counseling. At the time, I was hopelessly lost, confused and damaged emotionally. I felt a sense of relief to be able to talk with my Pastor because

I had no one else to turn to. Even my only girlfriend who lived in Columbia at the time had no idea how much grief I was going through. I explained to Him that I wholeheartedly believed in the vows that I made before God. And I would be distraught by going through a divorce.

After talking with me, my Pastor contacted the ex in order to talk with him. He wanted to get both perspectives on the marriage. A week later, I met with my Pastor again. I could tell by the look in his eyes that he really did not want to have this conversation with me. But it was his duty as a Man of God to inform me of what I was dealing with. My Pastor never spoke of the counseling session he had with my ex. And I never asked. But what he did tell me sent actual chills throughout my entire body. He said, **"It is time for you to leave. God understands the vows you made, but He does not want His child to be unhappy either. You need to take care of yourself and your children."**

The amount of weight that was lifted off me when he said those words were so profound, so intense. My Pastor (may he rest in perfect peace) tried so hard to hide what he was really feeling. For an instant though, through his glasses, I saw the flesh side of his expression. It showed the disgust he felt for the ex and what he had done to his family. I sighed a sigh of relief and thanked Pastor. Now, after all the signs I ignored, I believed it was time for me to leave and God would not be disappointed.

When I made up my mind to pack and go, I thought about our children and their emotions. I did not want them to think that what their father was doing was acceptable. My daughter should never believe she should stay with a man that emotionally, mentally or physically abuses her. My son should never believe that he has the right to emotionally, mentally or physically abuse women.

I remember my daughter, who was only nine years old at the time, asking me, *"Why is Daddy coming home so late at night?"* I could not figure out how she knew about that, but I remembered the alarm would chime every time the front door was opened. My only answer to give my child at that time was *"You have to ask your Dad that question"*. I already knew the answer. He spent his time entertaining another woman. He did not even try to hide it. Narcissistic people leave infidelity trails behind thinking that no one is smarter than them. If you have every dealt with a narcissistic person, you know what I mean. They never do any wrong in their own eyes. They are always right. It is either their way or no way. So, when I questioned him about it, I did not know what I was talking about... until I showed proof. Then, the response is 'whatever'.

I do not know if our daughter ever asked her dad why he was coming home so late. Knowing my child, she probably did. I probably was not around when she did. I just wonder if he was brave enough to answer his daughter's question.

**Me**

I supported you when no one else would
**Me** ... your friend

I was there when you had no one to talk to
**Me** ... your companion

I was there when your most intimate desires needed to
be fulfilled
**Me** ... your lover

I was there when you said, "Till death do us part"
**Me** ... your wife

I was there when I carried both of your seeds in my
womb
**Me** ... the mother of your children

So now after all these years, you want to do your own
thing,
Make new friends and be your own man
You disrespect me, lie to me,
Desire someone else when I am home taking care of
your children
And you expect me to accept your betrayal, your lies
and all the disrespect?
Oh no!! I don't think so!
Because there are plenty of men out there who would
love to have a woman like ... **Me!**

Confirmation came on Martin Luther King's Birthday in 2006. That day, my ex and I had a 'Come to Jesus' meeting regarding our relationship and marriage. He begins by telling me ***"I know you don't love me the same as when we met because I don't feel the same way either."***

At that very moment, I died inside. All of what I spent my life hoping and praying for in a spouse blew away like dandelions on a breezy summer day.

I let my ex continue to talk, pleading his case as to why we were not working out. I allowed him to dig his hole so deep he would not be able to save himself. While he was talking, I then understood why my Pastor said why it was time for me and my children to leave. Knowing the kind of man my Pastor was, it would have devastated him to even tell me what I just heard from my own husband's mouth.

In the midst of it all, I still managed to say ***"Thank you, Lord"*** under my breath because he unknowingly confirmed what my Pastor had already told me. As I sat on the bed - in a metaphorical sense - I was holding my bleeding heart in my hand after my husband stabbed me with his words. As the blood poured out, I began to feel a little lighter, as if my burdens were being lifted. I do not remember crying, but I do remember what I said to him.

***"You said you know that I don't love you the same as I did when we met. That part is true. However, you have it twisted. Truth is, I love you more***

***NOW than I did when I first met you. Why do you think I have been trying so hard to go to counseling to save our marriage? When you love someone, you do not fall out of love with them unless they never genuinely loved you in the beginning. But I thank you for telling me the truth about how you really feel about me. Now, I can do what I need to do to leave and move on with my life while I still have a chance."***

There was a great sense of empowerment after that statement. What the ex said to hurt me, motivated me even more. I just needed that P.U.S.H. moment and it was granted. God was leading me out of Egypt just like Moses did for his people. The sea parted for me and it was time for me to go. I left knowing the unjust will never prosper. Never.

## Questionable Love

How can I love someone that doesn't love me?

I did it.

It is nothing that I am proud of,

Nothing that I can brag about.

To be quite honest, I feel very dumb and naïve.

I was hoping and praying for change.

Maybe he can grow to love me.

Maybe being together can make him feel differently.

But I know better now. I am relying on You, God, to help me heal.

## Thank you, Girl

**Thank you, girl ...**

For the late night calls on his cell phone.
For keeping him all hours of the night when the kids and I were home alone.
For making him want *'some more of that'.*
For making him leave his family on Christmas Day.
For making him choose between his wife and you.

Thank you, girl, because WITHOUT you ...

I wouldn't realize the extent of his selfishness and lies.
I wouldn't realize how manipulative and deceitful he was.
I wouldn't realize how disrespectful he was to me and our children.
I wouldn't realize how naïve I was to believe that he loved me for better or worse.

Thank you, girl, because OF you ...

I can now raise our children by myself and teach them morals to live by that don't include infidelity.

I can now understand why he wanted you instead of me because of his own insecurities as a man.

I can now understand how truly stupid YOU are for getting involved with a man who cheated.

I can now say that you are not the 1st, 2nd, or 3rd woman to interfere in me and my man's relationship. YOU ARE THE LAST!

Thank you, girl! I can't repay you enough for all you have done TO me and FOR me. But I know that in time, God WILL bless me in the presence of my enemies!

Thank you, girl!

# CHANGE IS COMING

For the next the next ten years, the ex made my life hell on earth. He would always find a way to prolong the divorce by bringing up frivolous things to delay the process. In between time, co-parenting was terrible. Since I moved back to my hometown with the kids, I agreed to meet halfway for the children's weekend visits. But those kind gestures from me stopped when he would show up late. Sometimes extremely late. That is when I finally had to put my foot down. You want them for the weekend, come drive all the way to come and get them. I was not about to be used just to make things convenient for him.

When we finally did get divorced, he would never abide by to the divorce decree. It was his way or no way. By this time, I was sick of him and truly exhausted of his narcissistic tendencies. That is when I finally grew a pair and would not allow some things to happen. Although I never kept him away from his children, some days it was extremely hard not to.

Change was coming; it had to. I did not know it at the time, though, because nothing good ever came to me. Somehow, I was ok with that because my children were blessed. There were my reasons to keep living and that was all I cared about. I did not even care about myself at this point. My self-esteem and self-worth died little by little with every breath I took. I can only think of four momentous events that brought joy to me – the birth of my daughter, the birth of my son, my divorce and graduating from college.

Life for me personally at this point was meaningless. But I kept on because I had two young people that needed me. I had thoughts (that I know now were suicidal thoughts) running rampant in my mind that they would be better off without me. But then I realized that if I were gone, they would be raised by their father. I could NOT have that! Therefore, I had to press on and keep on living.

It was not until a Woman of God spoke life into my spirit in 2016 that I realized I had been holding on to ten long years of anger, resentment, bitterness, rage, and hate. I had to forgive the ex and more importantly myself. The time was now. Why now? I was not sure at the time, but I figured it out later. I had to purge the 'death' that was looming over my soul. All those difficult years, I was literally clinging to my life and praying that I would not let go. I was barely holding my head above water. However, it took this evening with her to release the demons that my ex had over me and the demons I had within me. My life would not thrive if I didn't. She told me that. I believed her. I cried... and screamed... and wept until I felt that heavy burden lifted. If you have never experienced that feeling, trust me ... it is a feeling like no other.

She even told me that I will meet someone that will give me the love I deserved. Well, at the time, I did not believe her because I did not feel deserving of love. I was just thankful for the peace that I felt. Around the time of my spiritual awakening, little did I know that the foundation of the "someone" the Woman of God spoke of was someone I had already started having conversations with.

About 9 months prior, I knew (but not really) of a man that I only knew through a mutual Facebook group. We only became Facebook friends because of this group, but we never had any kind of verbal conversation. I would only see his random posts on my newsfeed and that was about the gist of it ... which was nothing. This one day in February of 2016, I kept seeing different mutual friends posting condolences to this man for the passing of his wife. Even though I did not know him, I too gave him my condolences on his page. After I left my post displaying my sincerest condolences, I never checked to see if it was liked or even read. I had my own things going on and keeping up with posts was not one of them.

Sometime during the summer, I remember seeing an incredibly sad message written by this man about missing his wife. It just about broke my heart. I never lost a spouse, but I could relate to losing someone close. I reached out to him in his inbox to ask if he was ok. And I asked if he would be interested in a participating in a private group on Facebook I started that was dedicated to people who suffered from depression. He said yes. So, after I added him to the group, that was as far as it went with any conversation between the two of us.

A few months passed after that. This time, I expressed I was having a bad day on my Facebook page and he reached out to me to ask if I was ok. When he contacted me, I could not respond because I was on my computer at work so I asked if he could call me on my work phone (you know how it is ladies... never give out your real phone number until you know what kind of man you are dealing with {smile}). It was surprisingly interesting to hear him for the first time because I could clearly hear his Alabama 'twang'. Although he will completely deny any kind of dialect in his voice.

That was the beginning of a beautiful friendship. It was so nice to be able to talk to someone who did not know me, and I did not know anything about him. Neither one of us were interested in dating. Our main priority in life was all about taking care of our children. I was thankful for getting rid of my demons and he was still grieving for his wife while trying to raise a 12-year-old son. Our conversations were mainly about life, raising kids, grieving, working, what the future holds, etc. Besides, this man was two states away. If I could not have a meaningful relationship where I lived, how could I have one with someone long distance? So, the thought never crossed either of our minds.

The beginning of 2017, I took a hiatus from all my family, friends and social media because I was taking on too many distractions and not handling my own problems. I was severely depressed but managed to maintain my life day by day. I began to make plans for a 'great escape' from my job of eight years. The outright disrespect and challenge of my character after a new supervisor was hired caused me to want to leave a job that I loved since 2007. Since I started working there, I received 'exemplary' on every evaluation every year of my employment. I was good at what I did. One may consider it bragging; I consider it as confident. And very rarely did I give myself compliments. I even took on responsibilities I was not 'qualified' to take on. But I did it and did it well. However, it took one person to make other people question my work ethics and behavior. That was not acceptable to me. This was the year that I decided to take a stand for myself. No one was ever going to take away my peace ever again.

The only person I talked to about this was the man that became my best friend. He was behind me every step of the way. The entire month of February in 2017, I took a little of my belongings home every day. The only thing left to take were pictures from my wall. I informed my best friend of my plans to work up until mid-morning, not revealing anything to anyone. Then I left like a thief in the night. No one saw me leave. No one, that is, except the HR person I handed my badge and keys to. Once I was off campus, I emailed all my close co-workers to say my good-byes and I thanked them for the wonderful years I shared with them. And I thanked them for believing in me. These emails went to those who never doubted my character. All other co-workers ... well they found out from the ones I emailed. If I were a deceitful person like I had been accused of, I could have left my desk a complete mess. But instead, I had everything nice, neat and in order so that they could never say I kept that desk in disarray after I walked away. I left on MY terms. And I never looked back.

I am thankful for this man for having my back and trusting my decision. He never questioned my reasoning or tried to stop me from what God laid on my heart to do. My best friend ... he said, **"I got you"**!

## What's Wrong With Me?

Are my lips too thick?
Are my hips too wide?
Is my full figure too fulWhen I stand to the side?
Are my breast too big?
Is my waist too small?
Do you think my small legs
Can carry this all?
What is it then?
I don't understand.
Why is it so hard
To find me a man?
But I suppose the real question
Should really be,
Why can't a man
Be interested in me?
Is it partly because
My hair is not straight?
Humph! My body will NEVER again
See a size 8!
Is it the dark brown color
Of my forty-something skin?
And believe it or not
All of my teeth are still in.
What's wrong with me, Lord?
Is it destined to be?
Will the rest of my life
Be lonely for me?
It hurts so bad,

But I'm used to it now.
My self-esteem and self-confidence
Is way, way down.
But no need in worrying
About what I believe.
Because thank God in Your eyes,
There is nothing wrong with me.

# Something Shifted

After I left my job in March 2017, I decided to do things on my terms and in my own time. I never traveled a lot before, so I asked my best friend if I could come to his state to visit. I had never been to Alabama so this would have been a treat for me. Of course, he was shocked that I would want to travel that far and even more shocked that I would want to come and visit him. Besides, we never even talked about seeing each other – until now.

I have a fear of heights. Worse… I have a fear of flying. This was the day I had to take a whole anxiety pill for my nerves. I was sincerely about to face a fear … for a man I have never met. The excitement was there, but so was my anxiety. However, it was too late. The ticket had been purchased and plans had been made.

The moment I made my way down the escalator to meet my best friend, I was so nervous yet enthusiastic. When you think about meeting people for the first time, you expect the unexpected – you know, the unknowing. One thing I can tell you is when I first saw him, some 'thing' was there. His smile was electrifying. His warm embrace melted the wall I had built with mortar and concrete. But I did not go to Birmingham to fall for a man. I just came to have a great weekend with the man who kept me laughing until the wee hours of the night.

Our weekend mainly consisted of sightseeing, eating, and laughing. He took me to a few different restaurants that we did not have back in South Carolina. Eating was my thing! I know for sure I gain at least 10 pounds during the weekend. I had great company because he was just as humorous in person as he was on the phone. My last night there, we went to one of his co-worker's husband's birthday party. The way people were looking at us at the party questioned whether we were 'together'. It was not a date... technically. We were just friends who looked good together (smile). I was tickled every time I looked across the room and my bestie was staring at me and smiling. Me? Well, I would start grinning and blushing like a fifteen-year-old. When we danced, it felt like it was just the two of us there even though there were at least 125 guests in the room. It was so refreshing being treated and respected like a lady. And I mean genuine respect - no sexual innuendos, no sense of fear being out of my element, no lack of chivalry.

When it was time for me to catch my flight back home, I did not want to leave. I felt like I belonged there. My soul found a destination of peace embodied in the aura of this man. I did not understand how or even why, but I knew secretly I felt something for him. As my plane ascended into the clouds, I cried real tears. Yes, what I felt was real.

That weekend, something shifted.

After I made it back home, exhausted from an extremely long layover and a time change, I could not wait to talk with my best friend about our wonderful weekend. It was such a refreshing feeling being completely happy and peaceful.

But wait ... our conversations changed. What once was innocent talk about everyday events and life in general became "when can we meet again"? I must admit... I was so excited to hear him say that. Because the feelings were unequivocally mutual. We knew what we were getting into. Two states away and six hours apart, this was not going to be an easy task. However, we were both willing to make it work.

Even though both of our children were in school and we each had weekend obligations, we always found a way to meet at least once a month. After the initial visit, I went to Birmingham twice and he came to Summerville once. The rest of the time we met in various halfway meeting places. Each time, it was an adventure... each time, the feelings grew deeper... each time, it was harder to leave him and go back to our separate lives.

When we met again in May, I remember my best friend looked at me and said, "I am going to marry you." It just came out. No forewarning, no "Guess what I am thinking?" ... just a statement that really did not take me by surprise. I looked at him and just said 'Ok'. Thinking he was joking, I just kind of rolled my eyes and we carried on with our day.

On November 5, 2017, my best friend said let's go to the jewelry store. It was not problem because I needed to get one of my rings inspected anyway. When we got there, he was over in the corner talking with one of the salespeople and I was in the Chocolate Diamond section. It is always my first stop when I walked in the store. I'm making small talk with a salesperson while trying on a ring when I got a phone call from a friend of mine. She had just started talking when I was called over to the side where my best friend was standing. As

I was getting off the phone, I noticed the two salespersons were looking at me. My best friend told me to try on a ring. It was an engagement ring with a jacket. Caught totally off-guard, I was speechless and taken aback by what I thought was going on, but I did not want to assume. He put the ring on the third finger of my left hand and I said how beautiful it was. My best friend looked at me and said,

> ***"Wendy, I told you back in May that I was going to marry you. I am true to my word. I am standing here before you and the other people in our presence to ask you to marry me? And if you say yes, keep the ring on because it is yours."***

Unbeknown to me, the salesperson captured a picture of me and my fiancé in front of the store's picturesque board on the back wall as my best friend asked for my hand in marriage. The emotions that flooded my head and my heart could not be expressed into words. But my mouth did manage to say ***"Yes"***!

## Save Me Lord

**S**ad all the time
**A**lone and unloved
**V**alue seems unworthy
**E**nding with disappointments

**M**ake me an example
**E**nvelope me with your Glory

**L**ove is what I need
**O**rdained by God
**R**enew in me
**D**evine intervention

# I Do

April 21, 2018, I married the man God had destined just for me. The love of my life. He laid down the foundation of our beautiful friendship, then started building its sturdy walls day, by day, by day. And each day, He solidified the strength of our building, our very own stronghold. A building that no man can or will be able to tear down. Yes, indeed - God blessed me with my best friend.

We were married in Charleston, SC, in front the beautiful houses on The Battery. My husband tells everyone we had a 'Flash Mob Wedding' because we said our vows in front one of the historical houses near the road. It was the most beautiful, spur-of-the-moment places I could ever imagine. And because we were just that close to the street, we received several horn honks and congratulatory wishes screamed out of car windows. Our wedding party consisted of my husband's son, who was the Best Man, my daughter who was my Maid of Honor, my son who gave me away and my daughter's boyfriend who prayed for our blessed union. Our wonderful photographer did an excellent job capturing our moments in time. Those photos will forever be remembered and cherished. That day could not have been anymore perfect.

I felt in my heart that this union was the beginning of something wonderfully made just for me. Not just my husband, not our blended family, but a new sense of healing that God was placing in my life. And the reasoning was not plain to see before that time. However, as time went on it became abundantly clear...

everything I went through in life, I needed to go through just for this purpose. The purpose that I needed to fulfill and share with you, my readers. The love that I have been blessed to experience have made my vision so much clearer, my thinking so much wiser, and my purpose much more vivid.

# MY TIME TO LIVE

All my life, I felt like I was dying a slow death. From receiving no love from my mother, to being raped in college, to having a miscarriage at work, to marrying a man who did not care about me, to having doubts about a sibling no one would confirm the validity to me. I know God never promised an easy life to no one. I would be naïve to think I would be an exception. However, I learned that I had to die in order to live.

I am thankful that God blessed me to see a psychologist who helped me through some of the most difficult times in my life. She helped me by opening some of my wounds I chose to close too quickly. Together, as we re-opened those wounds and cleaned out all the nasty debris like resentment, hurt, and anger that I had left covered up, I was able to understand my mental state is the way it is. Underneath the wound was place that should have been completely medicated and healed before closed. She explained to me that my anxiety just did not start on its own. I have been through so many traumatic and stressful situations that I probably already had anxiety. It's just that my anxiety is more prevalent and noticeable now as I have gotten older.

My psychologist had to leave for another job position and when she told me, I felt like I lost my best friend. I cried. However, she left me with another wonderful colleague that has been tremendously helpful on my healing journey. I am so thankful for these women who have not only helped me to see my way through life's journey but are helping me to stay on course. I would recommend anyone who has to the ability to, please seek some sort of counseling. There are some experiences in life you just cannot go through by yourself. I did and it cost me years of unnecessary anguish.

A short time ago, I finally got up enough courage to talk to my Momma about my feelings growing up, the hatred that I felt coming from her and how all of that affected me from a little girl into womanhood. Her response was surprising yet somewhat unbelievable. She told me that when she was younger, when she was growing up, no one ever expressed 'love' languages. No one said *I love you*. So therefore, she either did not know how to express her emotions or she just decided to keep that generational trait. Well, I believe it was the latter because she knew how to express anger very well. After it was all said and done, she did apologize for making me feel that way for all those years. I thanked her, appreciated the apology and forgave her.

My mother, although she never showed me the love that I desperately needed, I still and always will love her regardless. She was the one who carried me and gave me life. Even when I felt that my life was not worth living, it was her (and God) who gave me this gift. So, it is up to me to take this opportunity to make the best of my time here on earth. I am still disappointed and hurt that after two years, she never tried to make an effort to come and see the new life I made with my new husband and son in Alabama. I cannot make her come ... and I won't. I will just keep loving her from a distance. That is all I can do. Therefore, I had to die just so I can learn that even the people who are the closest to me, they are not obligated to love me. No one is. First love comes from within, not from another person. I wish I had known that forty plus years ago. But the most important thing is that I do now.

In the meantime, I chose to break that generational cycle and expressed to my children how much I love them daily. Sometimes several times a day. They need to know from me that THEY are my blessings from God. God chose me to teach them the way they should go so that when they become parents themselves, they will not depart from the wisdom I gave them. So, I had to die just so I could know how to love my children unconditionally.

In college, I was violated in the most vile and unimaginable way. I have since learned to forgive myself for feeling like I did something wrong. I did not ask for him to violate me. I did not ask him to take away my spirit. Therefore, all the thoughts of blaming myself are now null and void. I can now understand that I had to die in order to live through being sexually abused. It was through that horrible experience I have gained resilience and strength I did not know I had. I hold in my heart that God has dealt with the man that violated me. Nothing good can come to people who do others wrong. I strongly believe that.

When I had my miscarriage, my baby and part of me died, too. But I had to forgive myself for the self-blame. God knows in my heart and in the depth of my soul that if I had known ahead of time that I was carrying life, things would be different. I still cry sometimes because the baby was never given a chance at life; never got to take its first breath. But I know now that things are the way they should be. God does not make mistakes. It happened the way it was supposed to happen. Even though we both died that day, I am strong enough to embrace the emptiness that I will never get back. And I can love the children I do have even more.

My first marriage/divorce was a slow twenty-year death that seemed it would never end. I take responsibility for my part in this lengthy demise. I have forgiven myself for all the blame I put on myself. I know that I did not deserve to be treated the way that I was, but I stayed when I knew better. I should have listened to my intuition (God), but I did what I wanted to do, not what God intended me to. I am still asking God to help me to not live by regrets because I was blessed with a positive product out of that relationship. It was two beautiful children that I am so overwhelmingly proud of. Because of his contempt for me, he has reflected it on both of our children. And it is such a shame. I was the one who raised them, but he will be the first to claim their accolades as part of his accomplishments; even though he was never around to help them when they needed him the most. I did not understand it then, but I do now. It is because of the ex and how he treated me that I now know what love is and the type of love I deserve ... something I NEVER received from him. So today, I want to personally thank him for being the type of person he is because without him, I never would have gotten to know what real love feels like and now I am blessed enough to live and embrace in it.

You are probably wondering about the little girl at the beginning of this book. Well, as it turns out, this beautiful, grown woman is indeed my little sister. A lot of people already knew or safely assumed. But after forty years of me being lied to about the paternity, after forty years of being denied taking part in her life, after years of my own children not growing a relationship with her children - cousins, I am horrified and ashamed. Even as of last year, I asked for the 'truth' and never got it. I never understood why we were never brought together by our parents. However, as you can imagine, we got caught up in an adult triangle and as little girls we were the ones who suffered the consequences. As I communicate with her now, I assured her that everything happened for a reason and God has a purpose. So, from now until life lasts, she is and always will be my little sister. We will not be able to bring back the years we lost, but I will make it my mission to love her profusely while I have a chance.

My love, my best friend, my confidant, my provider, my protector, my husband - my heart expands over capacity sometimes because of the love he covers me with. He showers me with adoration and affection every single day. He provides any and everything I need. He makes sure that I feel like I am the only woman on this earth. I never had that feeling - ever. It was always me making sure everyone else was good. There are times when I feel like I am suffocating whenever he is not around. God carried me through mental and emotional death just so I could have this beautiful man in my life and have it abundantly. And if God never gives me anything else in my lifetime, He has given me everything I need.

As I end this book, I want to leave you with some encouraging words. You will go through many difficult times. You may suffer several heartaches. You may get involved with someone who is emotionally, mentally or physically abusive. You may be called every nasty name in the book except a Child of God. There may be some days where life does not seem worth living. Or maybe it felt like you have already died. Know this... YOU were born to live your life no matter how challenging and unfulfilling things may seem. Every day will not be good. Every day will not be ideal. But you are perfect in God's eyes no matter what you are going through. You are here to serve a purpose. Do not waste any more time. Start living today.

Be blessed ... I love you.

## Beauty

### By Alexis Oldham

Beauty is the sun as it rises and sets,
It's the stunning sight of it reflecting off of the ocean,
It's the feeling of seeing the sun set and rise again,
Beauty is the sun.

Beauty is the moon as it is replaces the waning sun,
It's the light that illuminates the night,
How it lights the sky and announces night,
Beauty is the moon.

Beauty is nature and all of its portrayals,
It's the trees as they sway in the breeze,
The sound of the birds humming and leaves rustling,
Beauty is nature.

Beauty is the Earth as it revolves around the sun,
It's the place inhabited by human beings,
It contains both light and darkness,
It's the sphere of mortal life,
Beauty is the Earth.

Beauty is life and all of its perks,
It's how human beings connect with each other,
It's the hardships and pain encountered daily,
But it's also the love and happiness we express,
Therefore, beauty is life.

**This portion of the book is dedicated to you!**

**Since this is your private book, I want to you to use the next few pages to write down all the unresolved hurts, pains and disappointments that have not been healed. Even if you think you have resolved them, and it pops back into your mind from time to time, write them down.**

---

**After you have acknowledged some of the pain you are still going through, what do you want to happen to resolve these issues?**

---

116

**What are you willing to do in order to heal and/or forgive yourself? Are you willing to take the risk?**

www.ingramcontent.com/pod-product-compliance
Lightning Source LLC
Chambersburg PA
CBHW031302060726

47590CB00003B/1020